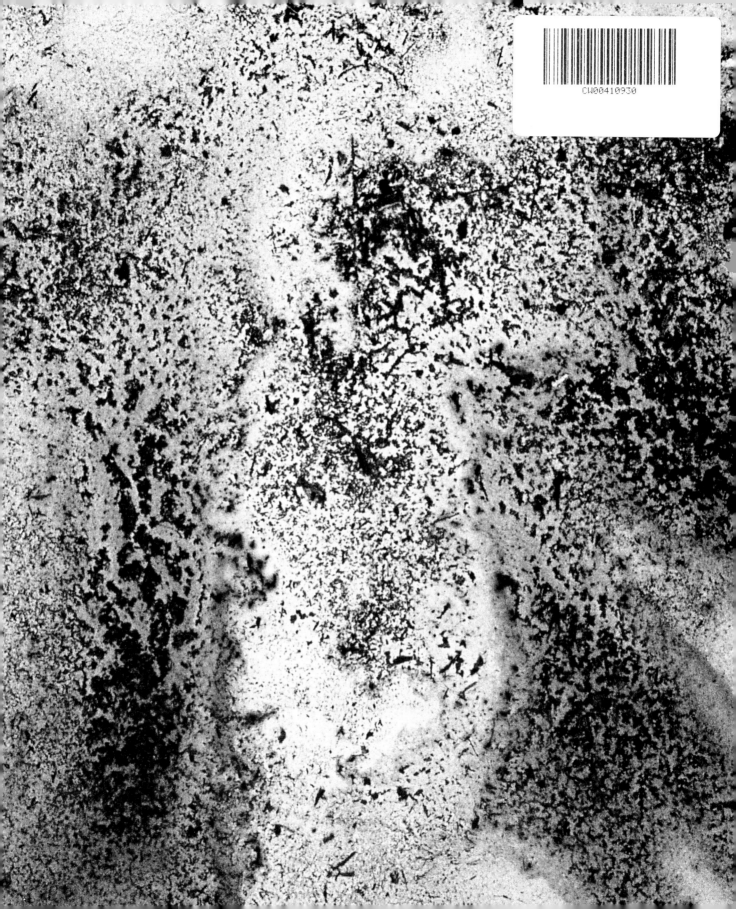

KING'S WOOD
beech, chestnut leaves, birch bark, blackthorn, alder,
hawthorn berries, Douglas fir, yew, blackthorn berries, pine needles,
Scots pine bark, Japanese larch bark, Norway spruce, western hemlock, oak galls,
western red cedar, larch needles, chestnut fruits, cherry, oak leaves.

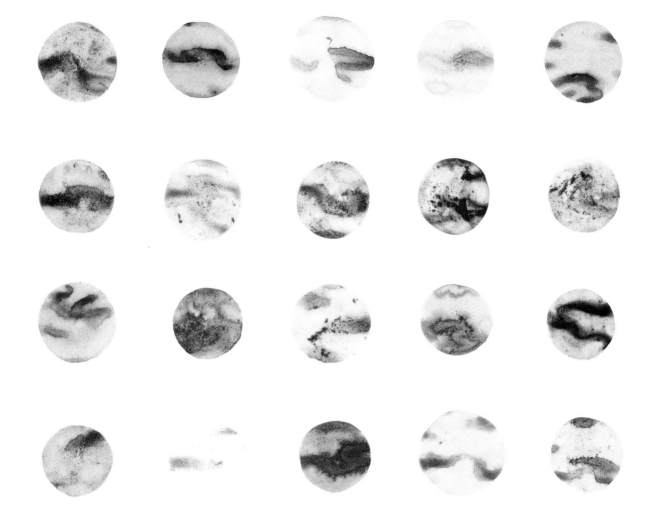

STEPHEN TURNER TREE RINGS

STOURVALLEY ARTS

PREFACE + ACKNOWLEDGMENTS

Sandra Drew, Stour Valley Arts

June 2003

Stephen Turner is an artist deeply interested in finding new ways of seeing the landscape. The new body of work in this publication emerged from his residency in King's Wood, Challock, Kent during a one year cycle, from October 2001 to September 2002. It was commissioned by Stour Valley Arts (SVA) as part of its international artistic programme. As with his previous projects, *Time and Tide* and *Tide Marks,* Turner has used canvases to record marks made by the surrounding environment in a continuing dialogue with nature.

In King's Wood he chose different species of trees particular to the forest and placed a canvas ring around each tree for a specific period of time which was determined by conditions and natural processes. The canvas rings were then left to the action of nature. They were marked from the ground below, from the tree above, by wildlife and the vagaries of the weather. They provide a physical record of each individual tree's unique ecology and symbolise the cycles of growth, decay and rejuvenation. These works have thus been made by the artist and nature in unison; as King's Wood itself, as a working forest, has been created by the action of people and nature together.

During his residency Turner also collected fruits from each tree (acorns, pine cones, berries), as well as leaves and bark which he steeped, soaked and boiled for their unique colours. From these colours he has made the tree ring drawings.

When considering venues in which to exhibit this work, we chose galleries which had an arboreal environment. Turner wished to create a tree ring for each venue which would be a work-in-progress during the exhibition and particular to that place. The Metropole Galleries on The Leas at Folkestone is set in a unique coastal environment and there is an evergreen oak on a step slope around which Turner has placed an almost vertical tree ring. The Natural History Museum in London was interested in collaborating with Turner and Stour Valley Arts as a way of making a connection with a habitat such as King's Wood. A tree ring will be placed around a tree in the Wildlife Garden at the Museum during Turner's exhibition there. At Tweede Natuur in Halle, Belgium, with which SVA has a history of collaboration, Turner has already laid tree rings in its forest landscape and will lay further ones to be concurrent with his Belgian exhibition.

This project and exhibition has contributed to Stour Valley Arts' increasingly rich archive of commissioned works. It has provided inspiration for educational workshops and revealed aspects of the wood and its ecology that may not otherwise have been accessible to so many people. For this and for being such a delight to work with, we thank Stephen Turner.

We would also like to thank the many other people and organisations who have assisted along the way. Forest Enterprise, with whom we work in partnership in King's Wood particularly Tim Gordon-Roberts for his co-operation and expertise, Jeremy Theophilus for his insightful catalogue essay, Martin Hall for his natural history notes, Dylan Woolf for studio photography, Dean Pavitt of Loup for design and Dexter Graphics for printing.

We are most grateful to the collaborating partners The Metropole Galleries, The Natural History Museum and Tweede Natuur, for facilitating the exhibitions and associated projects and would particularly like to thank Nick Ewbank, Sue Jones, Caroline Ware and Lia Schelkens. I would also like to thank Nicholette Goff for her work on the related education programme.

We gratefully acknowledge funding from Arts Council England, Esmée Fairbairn Foundation, The Metropole Galleries, The Natural History Museum and Kent County Council, without which none of this would have been possible.

Stephen Turner would particularly like to thank Steve Mace for his untiring assistance throughout the project and Sharon Clark for her help in the studio.

FRAGMENTS FROM A WOODLAND DIARY

Stephen Turner

[0]

The nearly full moon rose as I walked slowly through the trees and its grey light began to illuminate my way; contemplating ideas about transience, time and change.

Circular canvas rings placed on the ground around the trees could allude to the cycle of the seasons through their shape, and also provide a visible record of growth and decay. What will leaves, old bark, nettles, bracken, lichens and fungi do to unprotected canvas over a twelve month cycle? How will this vary tree to tree? How varied are the micro-environments of different trees?

A narrow deer trail heads off north from this junction. Will my canvas record hoof prints, the track of the adder I saw last week, or the fox from the nearby den? How many creatures will leave a trace of their passing on the circle? Leaf eating creatures, moths, weevils, aphids, leaf hoppers, lace wings, ladybirds, hoverflies, mice, voles, badgers, snails, spiders, beetles, earthworms, squirrels, jays, rooks, pheasant, wood pigeon, great tits, chaffinch, deer, centipedes, earwigs, woodlice, stag beetles, crane flies, wasps...

HOW TO ACT AS AMANUENSIS TO THE TREES AND GIVE THE WOOD ITS OWN VOICE?

In today's paper the narrowness of growth rings in Irish oaks was attributed to a catastrophe that struck the Earth in the sixth century. *"The trees are unequivocal that something quite terrible happened,"* Professor Mike Bailey told the British Association's Festival of Science.

Who else is listening to trees?

Notes toward a possible method - Tree Rings

[First select your tree.
[Clear the ground around its base to a diameter of 4m.
[Make a template of the trunk shape at ground level.
[Make a canvas circle (with eyelets evenly spaced around its circumference) to 3 or 4m diameter.
[Using template, draw the trunk outline onto the canvas centre. Cut out and slit canvas from edge to centre.
[Wrap canvas around the tree base and stake it to the woodland floor.
[Leave for 12 months (if possible) – equinox to equinox, an annual ring.
[Record at regular intervals.
[Stabilise, fix and remove from wood.

Making templates to record the different yet characteristic shapes of each tree's trunk. The beech, birch, fir, hemlock, red cedar, European and Japanese larch, spruce, sweet chestnut, yew and oak.

Cleared and prepared the ground to put the canvas rings in place. A new ritual act, to repeat for eleven different species – a particular portrait of the King's Wood. Ramblers walk by the yew as I work and ask why I am giving it a skirt. I tell them I am preparing a litmus test of the forest's health. Snottygogs, small red berries, immediately start to fall on the canvas – auto-arboreal drawing.

Chopped a path through five foot high bracken around a larch and placed a ring. A 'secret door' of woven bracken blocks the path and seals it from view; an arena for a private performance.

Feeling like a solitary hermit in contemplation of a newly laid ring of canvas around the Sweet Chestnut – a tree mandala.

[1]

Gathered different barks, seeds, leaves and fruits to test for colour. The rotting bark of the western red cedar is a deep reddish brown. Samples from different trees can provide a colour harvest. In the absence of many oak galls, made deep brown ink from acorns and oak leaves to a thousand year old recipe. Rich in tannic acid, it may burn itself through paper in around 300 years. Discovered spruce galls – aphids create a false cone. **WILL THEY PRODUCE A COLOUR?**

The studio is an alchemist's den: scraping, grinding, mashing, shredding, steeping, boiling, sieving, potting and testing. Colour studies pinned to the window, mellow in the direct sunlight. From peeled birch bark an orange hue; from straw coloured larch leaves, a crimsony red; lead into gold, renewal from decay, life from a death.

This King's Wood colour wheel has many closely related browns, orange and reds. At a time when technology can provide a near infinite choice of hue, less still feels like ineffably more.

Photographing each location to measure changes through the seasons. Yew circle 'berried', oak buried under a waving 'tide' of leaves.

Yew now has beautiful mottles all over the surface, with red lipstick messages charting human presence, white splotches mapping the bird life.

A Forest Enterprise tracked vehicle has crushed one half of the Japanese larch into the ground... **people have the heaviest footprints.**

Pink shell of snail shares oak canvas with an orange shotgun cartridge. Someone culling the deer perhaps, in this most managed of woodland. Save for a few remnants on Dartmoor, I doubt there is any truly wild wood in England.

'THE STRONG BASED PROMONTORY HAVE I MADE TO SHAKE, AND BY MY SPURS PLUCKED UP THE PINE AND CEDAR'. Wondering whether my pine and cedar rings might succumb to Prospero's storm on this wild and windy day.

Heard the story today of the disgruntled forester stalking an albino deer for 40 minutes in the evening light (when white colours really stand out). Moving slowly and quietly so as not to disturb it, getting close enough to shoot – at the chestnut canvas ring. Its white is now lost beneath a thousand leaves….
"Glory be to God for dappled things… fresh fire coal and chestnut fall"

Green blackthorn twigs give up blood red dye. Stirring a bubbling pot of it, whilst reading that Brazil was named after a tree that produces red dye – the Brasil tree. Found a few near forgotten colour recipes from pre Roman Europe and from the natives of north America, that all use trees found in King's Wood.

Looking for roots, leaves, flowers, bark, galls, fruit skins and nutshells to coax out their natural hues. I sometimes feel that the life of the tree is still present in the extract – the tree's natural juices, an elixir of energised colour.

Equinox Vernal 2002 +

(13.03.02 – 28.04.02)

Bluebells grow up through the beech and Douglas fir rings – pointy shafts puncture canvas weave, hungry for the light.

Drawing the birch, the chestnut and oak in sap from each tree, in a conceptual, emotional and devotional act.

Pine branches deposit needles onto the white canvas skirt, branches drooping down under the weight of gravity, but lifted at their ends by the attraction of the light...

...IS THIS SCIENCE?

A full moon, the woods full of sounds from children, scaring each other amongst the trees... [LUNATICS].

The moon governs tree growth. *'The diameter of a tree's growth fluctuates rhythmically in a double peaked wave every 25 hours and correlates strongly with the timing and strength of the tides'*. The creeks and runnels of the Medway, where I have spent so much time tracing the tides, have something in common with the trees of King's Wood....

Watching rainfall run off over the muddy ground in tree shaped patterns – how similar in form to the branching of the nearby beech trees.

Deer have scuffed up the edge of the **BEECH** ring, leaving some very fragile fragments in *splendid decay*. Pale straws, the remains of blue bells, still litter fragile cotton – their spring crown lost to the succession of summer growth.

Time to gather this canvas in, along with the **FIR, CEDAR, OAK** and **YEW.**

An ageing wild cherry sheds its bark to the slightest touch. Made rubbing onto paper from large fallen pieces.

So content working in the wood. Perhaps an occult connection from many moons ago still reaches out through some thread of DNA, connecting to a distant past when we all drew strength from the wild.

[4]

○

Remaining canvas rings taken in. The Japanese larch and spruce have been reduced to rags and tatters by the advancing armies of aspergillus mould. Ants have built a thigh high mound of leaves directly on top of the larch. Searched for two hours to find flimsy remnants of sweet chestnut canvas. Warp and weft of cotton, distressed by the warp and weft of time. Interfacing scrim may be needed to hold each one together, like the most delicate of ancient textiles... a relic of a wood.

Cleared leaves from the surface of the birch ring to reveal patterns and layers bedded into the mouldy canvas below. This is a record of what happens to the canvas as much as simply what falls on it. A lump of dung is near the tree trunk.

WHAT ARE THESE CANVASES? RINGS OF LIFE AND DEATH, ABSTRACTS FROM NATURE, OUT-TAKES FROM THE WOOD? LEAVES, TWIGS AND FUNGAL SPORES; INDIVIDUAL STORIES WITHIN UNIFYING CIRCLES.

What is a tree? To foresters it's a few pounds sterling as paper pulp; to the planner a lollipop in a concrete bucket and to the developer a name for the estate where the beech grove was. To many it's only 'a green thing that stands in the way'.

We live in a world where 'many scarce see nature at all', and need (at least) reminding of its great beauty and consequence.

This diary contains references to the following sources, in order from start to end:

The Tempest (Scene 5) William Shakespeare
Pied Beauty Gerard Manley Hopkins
Tree News Autumn 1998
'The tree which moves some to tears of joy is in the eyes of others only a green thing that stands in the way. Some see nature all ridicule and deformity... and some scarce see nature at all. But to the eyes of the man of imagination, nature is imagination itself'. William Blake

BEECH
Ø 3000mm
Beech bark, leaves, mast and twigs.
Blue bell stems, deer scrapes,
douglas fir needles, feather, mould.

TURKEY OAK
Ø 2500mm
Oak acorn cases, leaves and twigs.
Beetle remains, mould, moss,
pine needles, sawdust.
Tweede Natuur, Belgium.

PINE
Ø 2500mm
Pine bark, cones and needles.
Horse chestnut leaf, mould, moss, oak leaf,
sawdust, silver birch leaf.
Tweede Natuur, Belgium.

DOUGLAS FIR
Ø 3000mm
Fir needles, cone and twigs.
Beech mast and leaves, bird droppings,
bluebell stems, bracken, mould.

LARCH
Ø 2500mm
Larch needles, cones and seed.
Beech leaves, bracken fronds, mould, moss.

OAK
Ø 3000mm
Oak leaves, twigs and acorns.
Beech leaf, cherry stone, fruiting bodies
(common leafdisc), gun cartridge, snail shell,
woodlouse, wood pigeon feather,
yew needles.

SILVER BIRCH
Ø 2500mm
Birch catkins, leaves and flower cases.
Ash key, beech mast, bird droppings,
bluebell stems, deer droppings, dog faeces,
feather, mould, moss, owl pellets,
wild cherry stones.

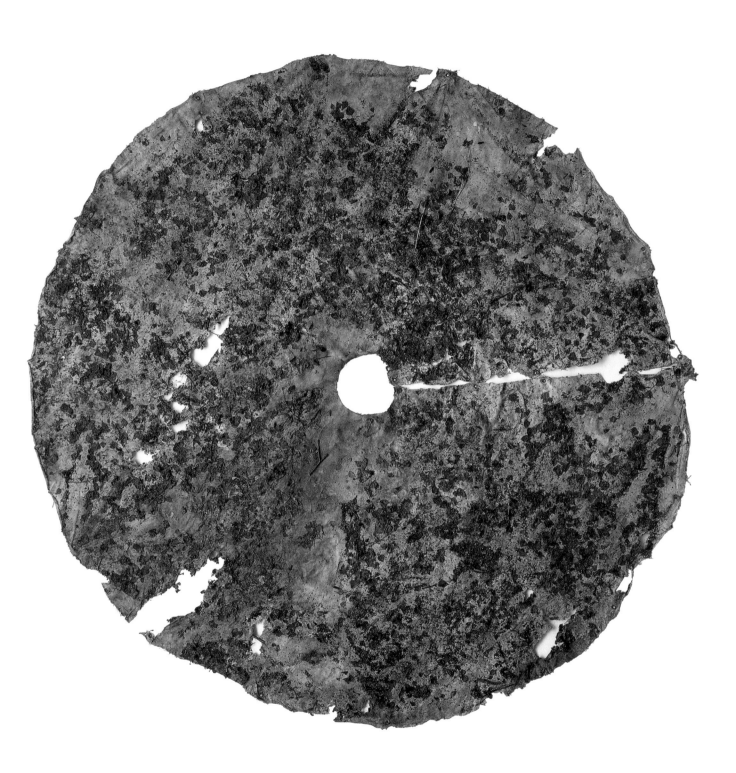

YEW
Ø 3000mm
Yew needles and yew berry stains.
Beech leaves, bracken, feather, lipstick,
oak leaves, small stones, woodlouse.

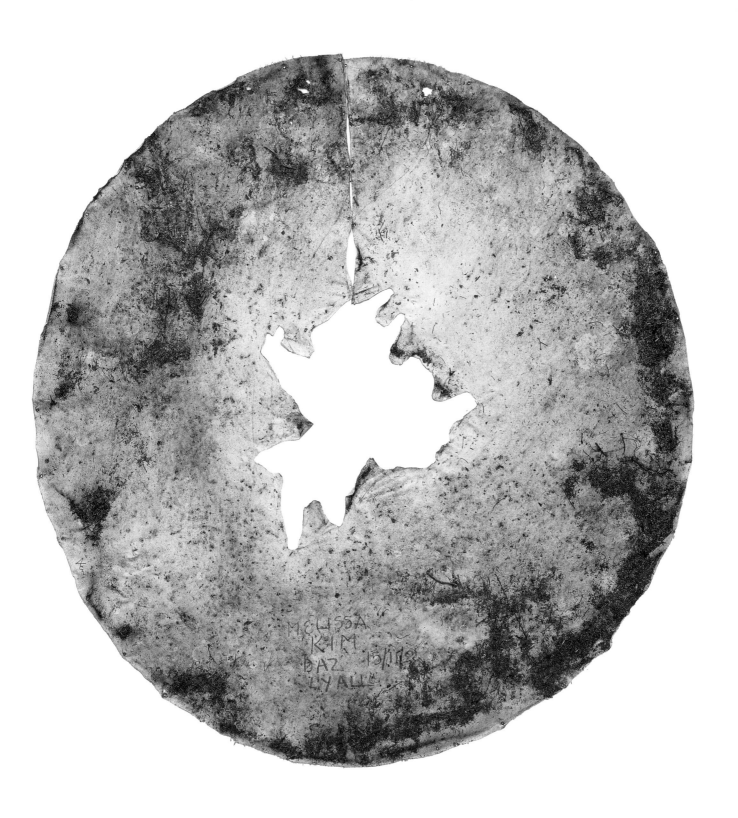

WESTERN HEMLOCK
Ø 2500mm
Hemlock bark, catkin, cones and needles.
Bird droppings, maple leaf, mould, moss,
silver birch leaf, sweet chestnut leaf.

INTELLIGENCE WITH THE EARTH
Stephen Turner: Tree Rings at King's Wood

Jeremy Theophilus

AS WE IN THE 'FIRST WORLD' are being forced to reconsider our place in nature, it is noticeable that artists are often being given a front line responsibility to restore some sense of a balance through their interventions into the environment. The history of Western art is a testimony to the artist's fascination with nature, from its earliest appearance in Egyptian and Roman frescoes, through the great flowering of the landscape as motif in the 18/19th centuries, to the Land Art of the 1960s.

A continuous dialogue then, that has both recorded and challenged our perceptions of nature; a process of documentation, interpretation and questioning. It has also been influenced by the changing character of patronage: from the church (wonder) to the aristocracy (possession) and the private and public collector (investment/self-improvement).

Underpinning this dialogue across the centuries has been a sense of reverence, of wonder, and more recently of acknowledgment that capture or control is fruitless and that partnership and balance are what will make continuing life on this earth ultimately possible. The practice of art itself has also changed as artists have extended the range of their curiosity and their levels of engagement with materials; the end product itself is often less obvious, its impact less direct and its function less immediately graspable.

As a consequence, a relationship with such work makes demands on the spectator that continue well after the direct confrontation: memory, association and just plain thinking are elements that help to fix or complete the cycle of creation, presentation and perception. The implications for this are that we as spectators need to bring not only open minds to engage with this process, but also a willingness to step outside our preconceptions of art and its processes.

The forest can be read as a symbol of nature's presence in all its apparently untamed state, an unknown and consequently frightening location; at the same time it can also function as a place of worship and of consolation.

Greenwood was not, then, like Dante's selva oscura, the darkling forest where one lost oneself at the entrance to hell. It was something like the exact opposite: the place where one found oneself.
Simon Schama – Landscape and Memory

For many people today it is another country, a foreign territory whose image is either based on a memory of nursery book illustrations, or the hyper-reality of computer games. Engaging with a tree in any meaningful way is increasingly confined to the urban park or the television garden makeover.

King's Wood is a remnant of one of the great forests of England: one early geographer gave the origin of Kent as *cainc, which in British signifies, a leaf* (Camden – Kent). The Wood contains a plantation of yew trees that are estimated to be at least a thousand years old. It has been a site of industry and human intervention for centuries, from Royal deer hunting to charcoal burning, from flint mining to tanning and house/ship building. It has survived alongside its human cultivators: nurtured and tolerated in equal parts.

Now, in the 21st century, the Wood is dependant as much on human recreation and creativity as it is on commerce: aesthetics and the environment meeting in an unexpected trinity with the trees themselves. And here the artist has become the new agriculturalist, re-interpreting the culture within nature and investing it with a new energy and offering a new opening for human communication.

Stephen Turner came to King's Wood with salt in his hair: his work over the past five years has been focused on the movements of the sea and the evidence such activity has left behind. His studio in Chatham Dockyard seems to exude the history of maritime activity: the former presence of engine oil, paint and rope combine to make a very particular scent. Now, as I write, the studio has become a laboratory for the results of his interventions in the Wood, its floor has taken on the appearance of the forest floor, and there is the smell of harvested elements of the Wood, fermenting and distilling in plastic jars.

His approach has been a simple one; to engage with the natural rhythms of the forest by placing circular panels of canvas around the feet of eleven different trees: white groundsheets cut to the shape of the trunks as they rise up from the ground, and pegged securely in place. The canvas then became marked, disturbed and even rotted by natural events over a cycle of up to twelve months, at the end of which each piece was carefully removed, with the "droppings" fixed in place. In some cases they were completely covered by the autumn leaf fall and required an archeological approach to the rescue of the original canvas and its most compacted layers. They were then laid out in the studio and more carefully secured and strengthened prior to exhibition, where they are pegged using offcuts from each tree.

Every four to five weeks Stephen returned to the Wood to document each canvas, keeping a logbook of text and images, rather in the spirit of a forensic scientist. And it is here that those tensions between intervention/creation and observation/deduction become most apparent: tensions that are both productive and challenging.

The panels that we see in this exhibition are small histories, slices of time manifested through the discarded parts of each tree. We have evidence of their particular identity, based on the certainty of falling and the random intervention of forest life, environmental conditions and occasional human intervention. Stephen is interested in that specificity, in drawing our attention to the individual tree, its unique character, and the discarded shadow of its past life.

Nature is so delightful and abundant in its variations that among trees of the same kind there would not be found one which nearly resembles another, and not only the plants as a whole, but among their branches, leaves and fruit, will not be found one which is precisely like another.
Leonardo da Vinci – *The Artists Course of Study*

The setting for a dialogue between certainty and chance, each canvas stimulates debate and hypothesis. The evidence itself can be identified and fixed within botanic discipline, but its location within what is, after all, an artificial space becomes significant in terms of both aesthetics and memory. The slowly decomposing presence of each fragment of the tree or, indeed, other neighbouring trees and plants, is part of its history.

It marks the end of a line that has traced both the ascent and descent of the structure and spirit of the tree. The architecture of a tree, the way it fills space in response to both its physical and climatic environment, and the way in which it creates its own habitat: these are all part of the implied narrative suggested by the tree rings. The juxtaposition of fallen fragments also "makes a picture", leaves us with an image which we will try to arrange within our own memories of the forest as well as using our "art eyes" to fit into other images we have experienced in a gallery. This ordering, which we do subconsciously, has been challenged recently in the growth of debate around chaos theory, and James Gleick has argued that
the essence of the earth ís beauty lies in disorder, a peculiarly patterned disorder, from the fierce tumult of rushing water to the tangled filigree of unbridled vegetation. James Gleick – *Nature's Chaos*

Notions of impermenance, fluidity and transience also come to mind when exploring these works, what Stephen calls "little relics of a happening". But of course this is a happening that is continuous, at many different levels, and these works serve as a reminder of cycles of life that underpin our existence.

The American artist Rachel Dutton, talking with Suzi Gablik before she and her husband disappeared into the wilderness to exchange artistic practice with that of pure survival, spoke of her newly acquired understanding:

It's like pattern recognition. I'd heard for years that in other cultures the things that are now called art in this culture were part of daily life. And this is one doorway into that. Tracking utilizes a huge amount of what art has been about only it's not a specialized, separate activity. It's something that allows you to be closer to nature and to realize that it all comes from nature. It all comes from the earth and we just rearrange things obsessively. Suzi Gablik – *Conversations Before the End of Time*

Part of Stephen's response to the trees, as with his work with the sea, has been to find a use for the material he collects, as well as representing his findings. He has made a series of drawings using inks made from each tree's own juices, as it were. Not only does this allow him to establish a visual representation of each tree, but it "makes use" in a way that echoes past users of the Wood, as well as the origins of artists' materials: Leonardo used oak gall as a medium for his drawings.

All of this helps to locate and preserve, albeit temporarily, a period of activity, a performance, that the artist entered into with the compliance of the trees themselves. It reflects the cyclical nature of the Wood which drew him into a similarly cyclical relationship, becoming in one sense reappropriated by nature, through observing, remembering and recording.

SHALL I NOT HAVE INTELLIGENCE WITH THE EARTH? AM I NOT
PARTLY LEAVES AND VEGETABLE MOULD MYSELF?
Henry Thoreau – *Walden*

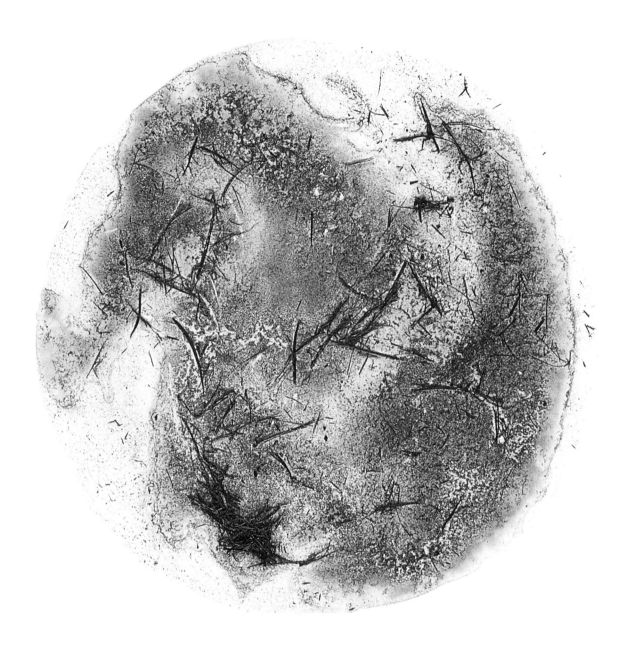

HYBRID LARCH Ø160mm *pale straw coloured needles*

BEECH Ø 620mm *leaves, mast, twigs*

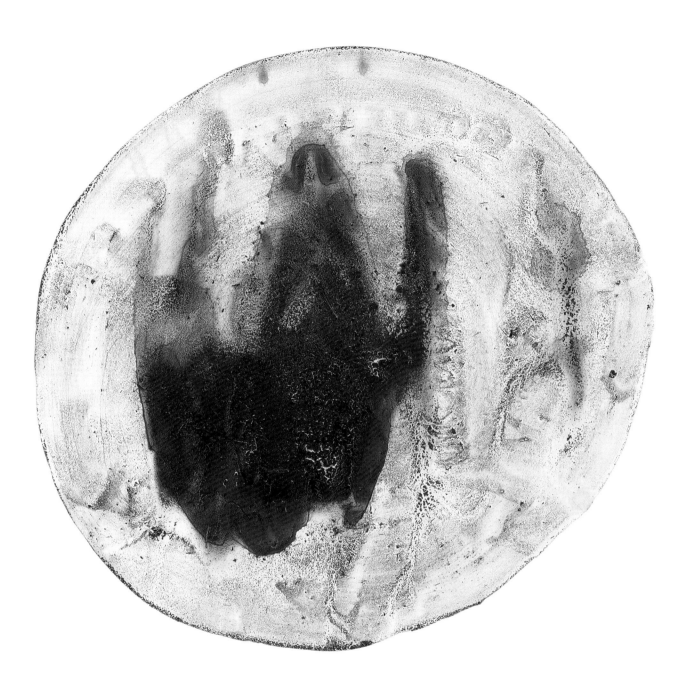

HAWTHORN Ø 610mm *berries*

LARCH Ø160mm *bark*

SWEET CHESTNUT Ø 160mm *fruit cases*

JAPANESE LARCH Ø720mm *cones and needles*

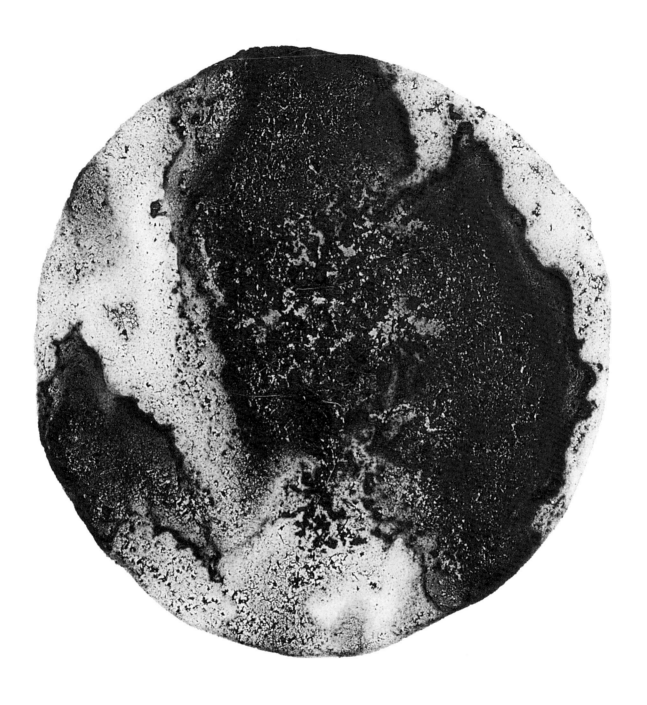

OAK Ø160mm *leaves*

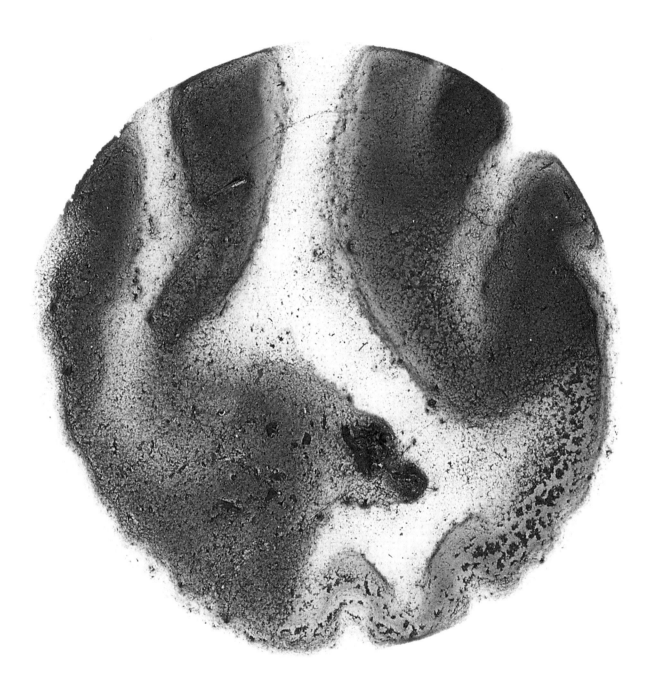

CHERRY Ø160mm *twigs*

YEW Ø800mm *bark, needles*

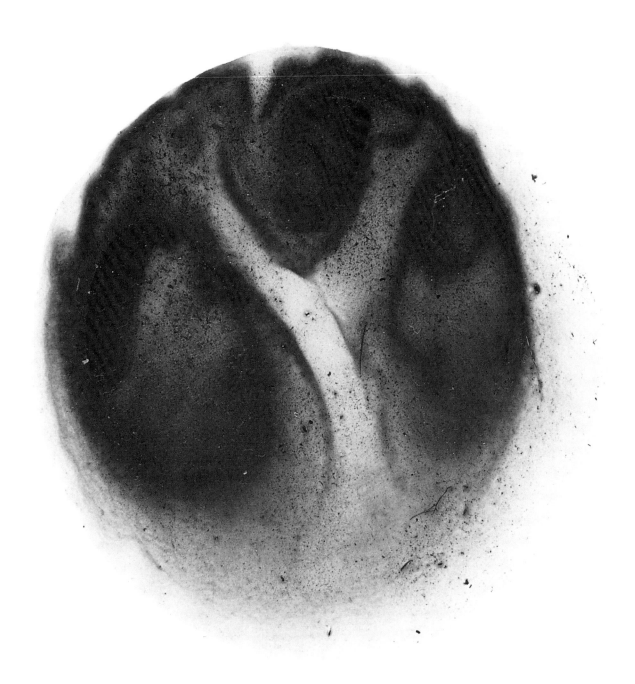

BLACKTHORN Ø160mm *fresh green twigs*

WESTERN RED CEDAR Ø160mm *bark*

METROPOLE GALLERIES
Folkestone, Kent

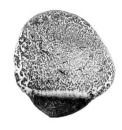

THE WILDLIFE GARDEN
Natural History Museum, London

TWEEDE NATUUR
Halle, Belgium

SITUATED HIGH UP ON CLIFFS overlooking the English Channel towards France, Folkestone's Metropole Galleries have two beautifully ornate art spaces showing ambitious, thought-provoking exhibitions of contemporary art. Commissioning new work especially for the Galleries' unique spaces and surrounding area is central to the programme, and a wide public is involved through activities which encourage debate and participation.

It is a great pleasure for the Metropole to be able to exhibit the remarkable series of works that Stephen Turner made during his Stour Valley Arts residency at King's Wood. In addition to showing the work produced during the residency, we have also been able to watch the progress of two canvasses placed around trees in Folkestone – one on The Leas near to the Metropole.

Staging *Tree Rings* has also given the Metropole the opportunity to begin to build a relationship with Stour Valley Arts, and I would like to thank Sandra Drew for making this exhibition possible.

Sue Jones, Gallery Director, Metropole Galleries, Folkestone

THE NATURAL HISTORY MUSEUM is the UK's national museum of natural history, and a centre of scientific excellence in taxonomy and biodiversity.

The Wildlife Garden was created as the Museum's first living and working exhibition. Situated in the southwest corner of the Museum grounds, it represents a range of British lowland habitats including woodland, meadow and ponds, and shows the potential for nature conservation in the inner city. The garden is fast becoming a haven for wildlife – over 2,000 species of animals and plants have been recorded since the site opened in 1995.

The garden also provides an invaluable outdoor resource for Museum visitors, volunteer groups and schools. Paths and boardwalks link the habitats, and during the spring and summer months visitors may observe some of the processes at the lower end of the food chain. School workshops are held regularly, investigating pond life, woodland plants and creepy-crawlies.

The Museum also promotes projects that interpret biodiversity in the Wildlife Garden using sustainable art forms. This collaboration with Stour Valley Arts provides an excellent opportunity to illustrate the character and ecology of trees using canvas to collect materials and imprints that occur through natural processes.

Through Stephen Turner's *Tree Rings*, we hope to illustrate an important link between art and natural processes, both in the Wildlife Garden and in the woodlands of southern Britain.

WHEN LIA SCHELKENS discovered a beautiful site in the middle of the woods outside Antwerp in 1994, Tweede Natuur was born.

Tweede Natuur (meaning, second nature) investigates the interaction of art and nature. Lia Schelkens works with artists to realise site specific commissions, both permanent and temporary. Invited artists create sculpture and installations mostly in natural materials, as well as making subtle interventions in the landscape itself. Since 1995 an ongoing programme of site specific works, inspired by nature and in particular the surrounding woods has involved many artists including David Nash, Sjoerd Buisman and Jacques Wirtz.

After meeting Sandra Drew from Stour Valley Arts (SVA) in 1997, an informal partnership began and various collaborations have since developed. SVA commissioned two students of Kent Institute of Art & Design, through the SVA Student Bursary programme, to make site specific work at Tweede Natuur in 2001. In 2002 Tessa Farmer's exhibition *Touchwood*, the result of her King's Wood residency, was shown in the gallery and amongst the surrounding trees. In 2002/3 Stephen Turner laid down three tree rings at Tweede Natuur, a work in progress, which will continue into 2004 and culminate in an exhibition. Tweede Natuur and SVA are currently working with the Dutch artist Sjoerd Busiman who is developing a project for King's Wood.

Now, after seven years as a private art and nature project, Tweede Natuur aims to reach a wider audience by developing further projects in various in public spaces.

Lia Schelkens, Tweede Natuur, Halle, Zorsel, Belgium
www.tweedenatuur.tk

Published by Stour Valley Arts,
King's Wood Forest Office,
Challock, Kent TN25 4AR England
T. 01233 740040
E. info@stourvalleyarts.org.uk
www.stourvalleyarts.org.uk

ISBN 0 9535 340 6 5

Edited by Sandra Drew
Essay by Jeremy Theophilus
Diary notes by Stephen Turner
Natural History notes by Martin Hall
Photographs by Dylan Woolf, Stephen Turner
and Sandra Drew
Designed by LOUP
Printed in Great Britain by Dexter Graphics

Distributed by Cornerhouse Publications
70 Oxford Street
Manchester M1 5NH
T. 0161 200 1503
F. 0161 200 1504
E. publications@cornerhouse.org

© Stour Valley Arts, the artist, the writers
and the photographers.

*Stour Valley Arts gratefully acknowledges
the support of Arts Council England and
the Esmée Fairbairn Foundation in the
publication of this catalogue.*

This catalogue has been published to coincide
with Stephen Turner's exhibition *Tree Rings*
which resulted from his residency in King's
Wood October 2001 – November 2002. The
residency was organised by Stour Valley Arts
and funded by Arts Council England, Esmée
Fairbairn Foundation and Kent County Council
with support from the Forestry Commission.

The exhibition is a collaboration between
Stour Valley Arts and the Metropole Galleries,
Folkestone, Kent (11 July –17 August 2003),
The Natural History Museum London, (2004)
and Tweede Natuur, Halle, Belgium, (2004),
with funding from Arts Council England,
Esmée Fairbairn Foundation, The Metropole
Galleries and The Natural History Museum.

Stour Valley Arts is an independent arts
organisation which aims to increase awareness
and enjoyment of contemporary art while
encouraging greater interest in the environment
through commissions, education, exhibitions,
publications and international collaborations.

Based in King's Wood, Challock, Kent
Stour Valley Arts has worked in partnership
with Forest Enterprise and other organisations
since 1994 to create a resource for artists,
teachers, students of all ages and the public.
A way-marked path leads to the many different
sculptures commissioned for King's Wood
which is open for visitors at all times. Stour
Valley Arts also invites artists to respond to
the forest using other media as with this latest
commission by Stephen Turner. For further
information about Stour Valley Arts at King's
Wood contact Sandra Drew on 01233 740040.

To visit the wood by car: from the M2 take the
A251 towards Ashford, from the M20 take the
A28 towards Canterbury and then the A251
towards Faversham. The Car Park and entrance
to King's Wood and the sculpture walk is
situated off the A251 at Challock, a half a mile
along the road to Wye.

Jeremy Theophilus is a writer, curator and
gallery director.

Martin Hall is an ecologist.

STOUR**VALLEY**ARTS   ARTS COUNCIL ENGLAND   The Metropole Galleries   ef Esmée Fairbairn FOUNDATION   THE NATURAL HISTORY MUSEUM   Forestry Commission